KUHLAU

MW00667778

SIX SONATINAS   OPUS 55
FOR THE PIANO

EDITED BY WILLARD A. PALMER FROM THE ORIGINAL SOURCES

CONTENTS

Sonatina Opus 55, No. 1 in C Major
    Allegro... 2
    Vivace... 4

Sonatina Opus 55, No. 2 in G Major
    Allegretto... 8
    Cantabile.. 10
    Allegro.. 11

Sonatina Opus 55, No. 3 in C Major
    Allegro con spirito.................................... 16
    Allegretto grazioso 19

Sonatina Opus 55, No. 4 in F Major
    Allegro non tanto..................................... 24
    Andantino con espressione....................... 27
    Alla Polacca 28

Sonatina Opus 55, No. 5 in D Major
    Tempo di marcia....................................... 32
    Vivace assai... 35

Sonatina Opus 55, No. 6 in C Major
    Allegro maestoso 39
    Menuetto & Trio....................................... 46

Alfred Music
P.O. Box 10003
Van Nuys, CA 91410-0003
alfred.com

ISBN-10: 0-7390-9855-1
ISBN-13: 978-0-7390-9855-4

Cover art: View from The Round Tower of the western part of Copenhagen
    by H. G. F. Holm (Danish, 1803–1853?)
    Watercolor, ca. 1837
    Bodil Bierring Billeder, Copenhagen

Friedrich Kuhlau was born in Hanover, Germany, on September 11, 1786, and died in Copenhagen, Denmark, on March 12, 1832. His parents moved to Hamburg while he was very young, and there he had the good fortune to study music with Christian Freidrich Gottlob Schwencke, the music director of St. Katherine's church. Schwencke had been a student of the famed Johann Philipp Kirnberger, who studied with Johann Sebastian Bach in the years 1738–41. Thus Kuhlau could boast of a direct musical lineage to the great Bach himself. He also had the distinction of winning the respect and friendship of Beethoven, whom he met during a visit in Vienna in 1825. On that occasion, Beethoven wrote a clever and humorous canon on Kuhlau's name, "*Kuhl, nicht lau,*" (cool, not lukewarm).

As a young musician, Kuhlau enjoyed a solid reputation as a piano teacher in Hamburg, and gave his first public recital there in 1808. Shortly afterwards, he published his first piano sonatas and several other works. In 1810 Hamburg was annexed to the French Empire, and Kuhlau moved to Copenhagen to avoid conscription into Napoleon's army. His success in Denmark was remarkable. He became a member of the orchestra of the Royal theater, and was allowed to present a concert of his own works. This brought such high acclaim that he was commanded to play before the queen. He wrote a great number of successful operas, and soon became known as "the great Danish composer."

In 1813 Kuhlau was appointed to a member of the Royal orchestra at the king's court, where he played flute as well as piano. For this he received a rather small salary, but was able to supplement it with his income from his many published compositions. Although he was never married, he retained a large household of relatives, for whose welfare he made himself personally responsible.

Kuhlau is still widely known for his compositions for flute, and some of his chamber works are still performed. His most valued works are his sonatinas for piano, which are highly valued as study material. These works, composed in the Clementi-Beethoven "legato tradition," are highly expressive, well-constructed works based on classical forms.

Sonatina No. 1
In C Major

Op. 55, No. 1

4

ⓐ The slurs and staccato indications in this movement are editorial. The original edition has none.

Sonatina No. 2
In G Major

Op. 55, No. 2

ⓐ Played: Measure 47 is similarly played.

ⓑ Play the small note very quickly, *on the beat.*

ⓐ Modern editors have changed Kuhlau's text to the following, to agree with the similar passage in measures 13 and 14:

We have retained the original version.

13

ⓐ Play the small notes very quickly, *on the beat.*

Sonatina No. 3
In C Major

Op. 55, No. 3

Allegro con spirito

18

Allegretto grazioso

ⓐ The small notes are played in their
written values, beginning on the beat:

ⓐ Play the small notes very quickly, *on the beat.*

Sonatina No. 4
In F Major

Allegro non tanto

Op. 55, No. 4

ⓐ This trill begins on the upper note. Measure 38 is similar.

Andantino con espressione

(a) *Polacca* is the Italian word for *Polonaise*. *Alla Polacca* means *in the style of a polonaise*. This particular composition retains a great deal of the Polish national style; much more than most selections with this title.

(b) The small notes are played very quickly, *on the beat,* almost simultaneously with the following large note.

30

Da capo al segno 𝄋, then Coda

Coda

Fine

Sonatina No. 5
In D Major

Op. 55. No. 5

Tempo di marcia

35

(a) Most editions have marked this movement legato throughout, which is certainly not according to Kuhlau's intentions. We have retained only the slurs included in the original edition.

(b) Play the small notes very quickly, *on the beat.*

Sonatina No. 6
In C Major

Op.55, No.6

Allegro maestoso

@ Played: Measure 82 is similarly played.

ⓐ Played: [music example] Measure 96 is similarly played.

Menuetto da Capo senza replica, e poi la Coda